Velvel's Violin

Velvel's Violin

Jacqueline Saphra

Nine
Arches
Press

Velvel's Violin
Jacqueline Saphra

ISBN: 978-1-913437-74-9
eISBN: 978-1-913437-75-6

Cover artwork: 'The Blue Violinist' (detail) 1947, by Marc Chagall © ADAGP, Paris and DACS, London 2022.

First published July 2023 by:

Nine Arches Press
Unit 14, Sir Frank Whittle Business Centre,
Great Central Way, Rugby.
CV21 3XH
United Kingdom

www.ninearchespress.com

Printed on recycled paper in the United Kingdom by Imprint Digital.

Nine Arches Press is supported using public funding by Arts Council England.

Supported using public funding by
ARTS COUNCIL
ENGLAND

For Granny Bessie, keeper of conscience
For Uncle Robbie, keeper of stories

*'Do not be daunted by the enormity of the world's grief.
Do justly, now. Walk humbly, now. You are not obligated
to complete the work, but neither are you free to abandon it.'*

– Rabbi Tarfon

Contents

THREE
SHALOSH
שָׁלֹשׁ

FOUR
ARBAH
עֶבְרָא

ZERO

EFES

סְפָא

Prologue

History becomes
Cassandra.

Done over
confused

she foretells
the past

and offers it
to the future.

As predicted
the project

is doomed.
The present

believes her
but doesn't

consider it
news.

ONE
ACHAT
תַחַא

'i can't go back
wherever i came from
was burned off the map'
  – **Melanie Kaye**

Tomaszów Lubelski

We found the family house
at least we thought
it was the family house

it seemed to fit
the description
but nobody knew

the exact address
and there were
no records

Should I knock
and ask for a tour
I was not certain

that request
would go down well
after all I might be

one of the Jews
of the recurring nightmare
wailing for reparations

prodigal returned at last
to reclaim
what was not mine

Where?

Not this England tight with inference
and understatement, the marriages
recorded, christenings and funerals
dated, graves traceable and visited.

Not this England: edgy, hedged,
and fenced; the safety of the tribe.
Homeland, border, territory, clan.

Open your mouth and taste the word *Jew*.
How it lurks uncertain under the tongue.
Now try *Belzec, Palestine, Diaspora*.

Anxious Jewish Poem

Jewish Brits are quiet, mostly hiding
under hats and breathing lightly
eagerly inaudible in Jewish whispers
stretched and tuned to bashful British
as Jewish Deputies doff their kippot
and stand to sing for king and country.
It's been a Jewish while since records of
a Jewish wave and you might say we're safe:
we pass for now, and some of us do not
observe, do not observe at all, but
Jewish who would trust the territory: its
Jewish folds and shifts, ancient slurs
that blur on, cringe and bleed through skin
of memory? Jewish history churns, red paint
spits the yids, the yids, Fagins, Shylocks, still
the Jewish money gags, nose jobs, sentries
at the gates. So keep your Jewish head down
and your Jewish bag well packed and when
push comes to Jewish shove, as has been proved
and proved again, my Jewish friends, however
Jewish you are not, they won't forget
your Jewish children and your Jewish god
your tarnished candlesticks, your stars
your rusty mazeltovs, your Jewish books.
Never assume. Accept your Jewish bread
unleavened; always be prepared to move.

Overheard on a Train 1

& all of queen victoria's kids
were rothschilds

sorry
that's wrong

i mean all but one

one wasn't

it's on youtube
rothschilds
nobody tells you that

Diaspora

I lost both my lovely uncles
one after the other
to another country.

Jubilantly they had passed
their examinations
and once equipped with

white coats and certificates
they poised to join
the gloried institutions

only to find corridors that reeked
of church and pork
of estrangement and handshakes

panelled rooms where their name
stuck to the roof
of the English mouth.

I lost both my lovely uncles
one after the other
to another country.

Just when we thought
we had arrived home
our shrunken family once more

found itself huddled over
indecipherable letters
despatched from distant possibilities.

I lost both my lovely uncles
one after the other
to another country.

On high holy days I spread
my grandmother's cloth
I lay out my mother's silver

and I miss my lovely uncles:
their blessings
and dreadful singing

their Jewish faces
blinking and flickering
in the candlelight.

Jewish People in the Area

Ephraim calls me on the phone before sunset
with a cheery *Shabbat Shalom*
Ephraim recently arrived from Brooklyn
   would love to meet other Jews in London

I do not know this Ephraim
and I would hang up
how did he get my number

but then he says
  I was sent
sent like a mini messiah
by my cousin Shimon the Hassid
to extend a hand and lure me
into the fold

   On the street in Brooklyn on erev Yom Kippur
   a Hassid and his teenage son seemed to know what I am –
     me with my illicit cone of Ben and Jerry's
     and they asked
   Have you heard the shofar today?
     to which I could only shake my head
   and the boy blew Jewish breath
   into the ram's horn for long, primitive, ancient minutes
   Cherry Garcia melting onto my shoes
   as the goyim passed by.

Ephraim, Ephraim
I say
        I need to be straight with you:
thank you for the call but I don't think
we have much in common
            Ephraim says again *it's just that*
I would love to meet other Jewish people in the area
and when we meet we will find something in common.

            The day cousin Shimon came to visit
            with his wife Gitl the wig-maker
            and his Parisian-chic mother Chana
            on a family matter concerning a disputed inheritance
            he laid his velvet pouch on the table
            along with a gift of kosher chocolates in great quantities
                – and truthfully I was dubious
                who has ever known a good kosher chocolate? –
            and the talk of money got all mixed up with
            Shimon's mother weeping in her mink stole
            eighty years after it happened
            Shimon's mother Chana
            who would not accept even a glass of water from my kitchen
                    as she told the tale of the French family
                    who sheltered her as a child
                    all the years of the war and how
                weeping weeping
                    she never saw her parents again

I tell Ephraim: I am far too secular for you
I don't even believe in God
you would not like my kitchen
I have eaten bacon
            Ah, that's okay – we have all shades in the community
            We are all Jews

When Shimon and I had come to an agreement
regarding the inheritance
he unzipped his velvet bag
with a quick invitation
to the only other man in the room

He helped my husband wind the tefillin
and place the phylacteries
and they said the blessings
in front of the women

    while I considered our non-existent god
    who abandoned a girl of three
    to hide for years in a stranger's attic
    not allowed to cry
    while her mother and father were slaughtered

    and I recalled
        Great Aunt Malka's tasteless kosher chicken
    her legendary cannon ball kneidlach
        she who had journeyed
    through displaced persons' camps after the war
        from Siberia to Paris where my family
        made a go of it trading in shmattes;
    my late Great Aunt Malka who had never
        made a will
    thus occasioning this familial visit
        and an awkward inheritance.

And after Shimon had departed with his wife, his mother
and her ancient tears
    I pondered the box of kosher chocolates
      said a half-remembered *brocha* for Malka for Chana
      but mostly for the chocolates
and let them melt one after another on my tongue
    and they were surprisingly good

Ephraim is still insisting
he just wants *to meet other Jewish people in the area*
and I tell myself
    he is a stranger in a strange land
    and surely I could ... and surely we are ...
but still all I can say is
    thank you yes
    I have your number and if
    I have time I will call you
I will call you Ephraim
    other Jewish people in the area
Ephraim yes I will call you
    would love to meet
I will
    I will
      goodbye goodbye

Poland, 1985

And the facades of Warsaw bared
their scrubbed-up skins; liveried waiters

offered nothing on the menu; bath water
rusted; the country roads were calm

a past I sought long overgrown
the state of currency still volatile

human traces vague, all guesses wild.
Nothing left to find; nothing and no-one.

But oh, the language: soft-tongued
apologetic; those legends of tracks

pointing towards infinity; haystacks,
horse-drawn carts; disappearing villages

where elders with wizened sensibilities
surely hungry for redemption would

offer water, sanctuary and bread.
Perhaps they remembered. Perhaps

going about their rural business
they thought of all those trains; night

and day, the passing of human freight.
But then again, perhaps not.

vintage führer

you can bid
for his face
on ebay
emblazoned
on an ashtray

Oświęcim

The weather hotter
than anticipated

the only drink
warm Coca Cola

the only food
dimlit eggs

with dark
indefinable sausage

and my father
red-faced

after his encounter
with a sweating man

in the canteen
who offered

a tempting exchange
for his dollar

a sheaf of zloty
interleaved with

(as it turned out)
joke banknotes

a bit of a blow
for us Jews

who'd voyaged
yearning across history

braced for a kind of
reckoning

a laying to rest
a joining of hands

as if

Bavaria

Today's news of war settles
as if boarding one of the latest trains

lacking compartments
disordered.

The view must always be sideways.
Nobody can see ahead.

I never know where I am
I know only whom I love.

I know this as clearly
as the clear river that sings

through the Bavarian town
I visited last week where

despite the shock
of language and lederhosen

I could assure my grandmother
she might safely alight.

Remember to wear the yellow shawl,
I could tell her.

Enjoy the small station.
No need to flinch

at the man with whistle
and uniform, together

we can walk these streets
where not much happens anymore.

You are not forgotten,
I could tell her.

I carry my loves everywhere,
faces lined up like little suns.

The train keeps moving
through the fog.

I gather about me
all that is good

like this reckless yellow shawl
passed down

by my grandmother
who bought it in Switzerland

for the price of a month's wages
just after the war.

o god

the trees are so tree
      the birds are so bird
          o god
even the green is obscene
           in its flaunt
and the tease of the breeze
the flagrance of fragrance
o god it's outrageous
      the sing of the spring
can I make you a list?

      hello?
     god, are you there?
  o god
o my god!
     it's almost as if
I believe
    you exist

TWO
SH'TAYEEM
שְׁתַּיִם

'And my scream is made of strange edges
like a complicated key'
  – **Yehuda Amichai**

Jew

a word that wriggles on the tongue; honey, beast and
almond, the soup of the afflicted, the wanderer,
the tailor, usurer, the book, the beard, the flat-cap
communist, capital conspiracy, the ducat and the lamb,
the red sea parting, slaughter and the slaughterer, the
ones who pass, the ones who don't, the nose, the noses

no, don't speak of those

the ten plagues, keeper of the Word, the shabbos hats,
the shtetl and the noise, the silence and the Sunday
luncheon tongue, the chicken head, the chicken feet, the
yellow chicken fat, the yellow star

no, step away, not them, not that

the interloper, interleaver, interbreeder, sadist bomber,
the broken glass, the kosher red, the Reb, the dross, the
shekels and the silver and the arcane script, the pointer,
the art of secular, the swastika

but why go there, don't go there

the dispossessed, the voyages, the drowned, the candles
and the soup of dread, the dread of soup, the trains, the
dead

don't dwell on that again

the chutzpah, chuppah, the marriage and the get, the
herd, the minyan and the Chosen

no, don't use that word

the shabbos challah and the oven, deep soup of despair

no, there's too much inference in there

the Nobel and the intellect, the where, where, not here, diaspora, the klezmer, mazeltov, the shabbos bride, the candlestick, the yiddishkeit, the pogrom

no, too grim, too grim

the tribe, what tribe, whose tribe am I, the exodus, the shabbos goy, the sheitel maker and the synagogue, the bagel-meister, lox, messiah, grave-digger, the mark upon the door, the vengeful god, the smoking tower and the big black boot

what did I tell you? leave that one out

the blintze, herring and gefilte fish, the just god, no damn god, the circumcision and the guilty god, the innocent, the pelt, the golden calf, blood sacrifice, the millionth Haggadah, the freedom and the desert blooming, the grind of the no-goodnik heart, the loss, the loss, and the broken homeland, kissed and coveted and lost, the uniform, the gun, the camps, the mortar and the gun, the firing squad

no no, move on, move on

diaspora, diaspora, the song, the song of sanctuary, forgotten song, the broken tongue, what song, what song

To the Ones Who Pass

Lately I have taken
to venturing a
   Mazeltov!
where others might try
   Congratulations!

Jewish fool! I hear you cry
   you never know
   who's out there
keeping an eye

The Plagues are Everywhere

Passover 2020

We gather round the plate, its song of songs
the history of birds on lilt and loop
of leaf and bloom, a blue of painted spring
to celebrate millennia of hope
against erasure. Did I say *we gather*?
Each in our little space, we make a grid
of faces. I feel I've loved you all forever.
For now, this is the closest we can get.
We work our shaky melody, we bear the weight
of memory and just for now, we're not alone.
The plagues are everywhere. We tell it straight,
we truly know it now. We fill our lungs
inhale some joy, exhale a kind of unison
singing with blue birds on a china plate.

Overheard on a Train 2

& gluing themselves to the roads
to save the polar bears
& bloody trees
& guata-bloody-mala

not

you know who it was
paid them to do that
george soros

george soros

nobody tells you that do they
I can send you a link
what's your number

Going to Bed with Hitler

After 'Hitler: A Biography' by Volker Ullrich

Most nights I can't wait to go to bed
with Hitler. Here on the low table
he squats impatient beside the lamp
that burns to illuminate the page.

Sometimes as I lie in bed with Hitler
his detailed obsessions bore me to
death and my eyes begin to close.
It is always at that moment that he
plunges forward and smacks me in
the face. *Achtung!* he says *You know
where this is going.*

How can I go to bed with Hitler? I
must be out of my mind: the weight
of him!

Nevertheless I go to bed with Hitler
every night as recommended by
my clever friend. *This book is a real
page-turner* she said *but do take care to
place it cover-down between readings.*

I am lying in bed with Hitler on my
chest and he is young again. We
travel to Bayreuth in 1925 and pass
our days with his dear friend Winnie
Wagner. Hitler is transported with
joy. *The sky was hung with violins*
he tells me afterwards *I had not a
care in the world.*

So there I was in bed with Hitler and it felt almost tolerable, but when I grew sleepy and attempted to put him down, he threatened me with bride school. *Kinde Küche Kirche!* he said, waving his fist.

I wonder if going to bed with Hitler could be profitable. For example, I could demand reparations based on his considerable royalties from Mein Kampf. *Have them; I don't need any* says Hitler *I live like a bird in the wild.*

I may be the first woman to go to bed with Hitler and put it in writing. Even you know now.

Recently when I went to bed with Hitler I found Martin Luther in his funny hat all cuddled up beside him. *Burn down their synagogues. Toss them in fire and pitch. Throw in some hellfire!* thundered Luther. *Amen* said Hitler. Surprisingly.

Going to bed with Hitler early on, I found I was permanently sleep-deprived due to his frequent and triumphant expostulations. *Blitzkreig!* he yelled at irregular intervals *Blitzkreig!*

Going to bed with Hitler is like sticking pins in my eyes.

Every time I go to bed with Hitler I grow gravid with information enough to vomit on Goebbels and his rhetoric: *The entire people love him, because it feels safe in his hands like a child in the arms of its mother.*

On occasion when I'm in bed with Hitler he shares his strategies for effective leadership. Let the minions squabble for power and approval; let the minions do the logistics; let them actualise my intentions; let them take the punishment for crimes and errors.

After a short recuperation break I just had to go back to bed with Hitler. He couldn't wait to tell me all about his victory tour of Paris and Napoleon's tomb. *The greatest and finest moment of my life!*

Going to bed with Hitler and writing about it is a risky business. You never know what people will think.

One night I went to bed with both
Hitler and Goebbels by mistake.
I lay still as death between them,
trembling under sleepless sheets.
*Magnificent how the people are
awakening*! Goebbels announced to
me, eye to eye, not realising he was
in bed with a Jew.

Some nights when I am in bed
with Hitler I try to tell him tales
of my murdered ancestors from
Tomaszów Lubelski and Aniksht.
I share photographs of Stalingrad,
Dresden, Bergen Belsen; but Hitler
turns away and busies himself
with strategies and calculations.

Why do I go to bed with Hitler
when I could go to bed with
Amichai who lies cast aside and
lonely on the low table beside the
lamp?

Apparently I will always be in bed
with Hitler. It's another kind of
punishment I inflict on myself for
being a Jew.

I spend so much time in bed with Hitler that he forgets I have a memory and merely forbids me to open my notebook. *The scream of the twelve-inch shrapnel is more penetrating than the hiss from a thousand Jewish newspaper vipers!* he shrieks.

I can't stop myself going to bed with Hitler and his late-night rants and furies, even when my heart falters and my lungs fill up with night.

I was in bed with Hitler trying not to disturb him with my breathing when he turned and shook me: *Are you the Jewish Bolshevik intelligentsia?* he hissed.

Finally, as I lie in bed with Hitler he begins to collapse in my hands. I try to explain he is losing the war. *Surrender now to save more bloodshed* I suggest. He smacks me on the face once more.

I continue to go to bed with Hitler despite the bruises. His face is grey as ashes; his hands are in a constant state of agitation. He rises up and extends his right arm. *Never Forget!* he cries.

These days I find myself going to bed with Hitler without even realising. I've given up all attempts to put him in order or put him away. I understand that he is not returnable.

But is going to bed with Hitler even sustainable? He is bent over like an old man. He's so heavy, the words are beginning to fall from his spine. The pages keep slipping and time loses all meaning.

In bed with Hitler close to the end, I turn off the lamp and drift off to the perpetual stink of finales: oily smoke, dead dog, diesel fuel and cyanide.

The Trial

'I didn't contribute anything to it, other than standing guard.
But I was forced to do it, it was an order'
— Bruno Dey, former SS Guard at Stutthof Concentration Camp

Slipped under the radar, back pages, smart
embattled, the old man shrinks and mopes
in his wheelchair. Justice has been halted
and restarted like a bad car; it chokes
on its own gas. This is not a time to share
more Jewish news, some might say; the trial
of a Nazi in his *autumn years,* papped here
face hidden behind a bright blue file.
The wheels move slow, it's getting late;
the perpetrator's half-asleep, doolally
propped up in the back beside the greasy body
of complicity, desperate and fake
knowing that history, that slimy bureaucrat
can turn. Our fallen statues tell us that.

Family Tree

The latest book squats on my desk
its typeface blurred

as if something wet has fallen
on the page.

It opens wide, its paper tongues
rehearse the words.

It waits for my silence
so I might hear it speak.

I tell my ancestors
now is not the time.

I am miles and decades
from that particular pit

awake in the buzzing hell
of an electric century.

I tell them this, although I know
they will not hear me.

I ask:
what can you teach me?

But they cannot care
about themselves or me

or the aftertimes,
they did not bequeath me

even their names
so why dig up the ancestors now

why exhume
their unborn tomorrows?

They lie where they fell:
thoughtless, tongueless

in some pine-filled forest
their bones

in perpetual embrace
with other bones.

Jew: the word is worn and haggard
even the trees

are weary of it.
I must let the word go.

Even the trees lie down
and weep; the forests are burning.

Mornings I wake with ashes
in my mouth

a half-remembered *Shema*
rolling from my tongue.

THREE
SHALOSH
שָׁלֹשׁ

'Death could drop from the dark
As easily as song'
　　　– Isaac Rosenberg

Before the War

for Nora Nadjarian

Dear Nora, we first met glad and unthreatened. That was before the war.
The book was open, the poem beckoned, but that was before the war.

My hair was probably straight, you told me, back when mascara mattered
and we were poised to write into every second. Such plans before the war!

Dear Nora, then death visited your father. But I must not say that.
The above letter was shredded; maybe that was before the war?

Today I saw the photograph of a dead man dumped naked in a well.
Grief still there, still there, you mentioned: of course, even before the war.

Dear Nora, remember when we talked about the moon and death?
I love to be alive! I offered. Life was strangely pleasant just before the war.

Writing for posterity: what a joke, you wrote. The poem held its tongue,
half-formed, half-present, muted by horror, not like it was before the war.

Grief is on its long, slow journey: an old man walks down a burning street
under the moon's dull crescent calling a child's name as if before the war.

Now truth drags out its death drawl: 'To which current war do you refer?'
We live in the dark of that question: no such era as 'before the war'.

Dear Nora, help me. The poem asks the poet: 'What rhymes with sorrow?'.
I'm too far gone to answer. I thought I knew. That was before the war.

'The Moment a Russian Helicopter is Shot Down'

I do not want to
        want to see this

For god's sake
        I'm a pacifist

I watch it eighteen times
        then put it on my favourites list

Tank Taunt

Hey clanking tank
     what lanky boys
grow in your belly?
       Talk to me Tank.
Lost your swagger and your swank?
   All splat and tarnish
eyes gone blank
   you're just a metal vessel
for the weapons racket
     won't talk back.
Do you feel pain?
       Are you outflanked?
 I hope you like to burn, Tank.
You can't turn back
   still taking orders from the man
who'll never thank you
    and to be frank
you stink a bit
     of murder, Tank,
one among the ranks of terror
   spitting death on children, Tank
     unchecked, untracked
and here you go again
      letting someone's rabid sons
still soft and green and clumsy
       with the guns
press all your dirty buttons, Tank.

Mercy

Today a crowd in consternation
tried to save a lone coot
from attack by apparent kin –
neighbours intent on territory.
A nearby fisherman lent his net
and a passer-by scooped her up
feathers and all, and lifted her
bleeding, onto the quay
to the cheers of the crowd.
She was half dead already.
We did not want enough
to do the merciful thing.
We had errands to run.
We dumped her under a tree
and continued on our way.

Yom Kippur

By afternoon I am hallucinating
salted caramel which is good for poetry
                because nobody wants implacably sweet
        in this age of irony and now they tell us salt
                        won't clog our hearts after all so maybe
it's okay that today, as the godless
        cycle in secular joy round the car-free streets
                of Jerusalem and hungry Jews everywhere
grow increasingly bad-tempered, I still
                        hold these grudges; lovely stodgy lumps
        at the bottom of my empty atheist stomach
                        although I no longer remember why
    and cannot therefore advise my son
                to prostrate himself before Justin Bieber
        for insulting him repeatedly on Twitter,
                        or my daughter to sweetly forgive
those girls for guessing her password
        and reading her text messages especially
                        considering my own sins are so old
        and wide and manifold and even as the salt
                is drying on my lashes I cannot bring myself
                        to say sorry to my own dead mother whom
    I should have venerated, but once told
                        to fuck off out of my life, or to a lost friend
who, even now, I dare not name, upon whom
                I may or may not have once inflicted
        terrible wrongs I cannot even now recall
                or to the children drowned near the shore
to whom I give scant portions my morning
                in momentary horror or for the promises
        I may or may not have made to polar bears

and nameless multitudes and I must atone
for the sins of my people
whoever my people are even though
I must atone
goddamit
as if it makes a difference
for my trespasses, omissions, misdemeanours
I must return to the home of my soul
wherever that is,
the home I cannot find
however hard I pray

Overheard on a Train 3

& did you know
there were more than
six thousand Jews
with offices
in the twin towers on nine-eleven
it's on record
& guess what
not one of them
turned up for work that day
i mean jesus
just saying
there's evidence
look here's a video

Velvel's Violin

After Rachel Shtibel

All the years of the war, Velvel's violin lay silent
under the walnut tree where he'd buried it.

Like Rachel and Luci, their childhoods gagged
in barns and bunkers, all it wanted was to play.

Their zayde witnessed, from behind the fence
at the cemetery, his wife buried alive by the Gestapo.

The graves are moving, the graves are moving!
he told the ghetto, and lost the will to live.

When Rachel and Luci crawled out of the hole
they'd shared for two years, they had lost their voices.

After the war, the remnants of family disinterred
Velvel's violin from underneath the walnut tree.

It is all we have left of Velvel said their father
but of course nobody knew how to play it.

War Games

Despair is the parcel
we pass amongst us.

Round and round it goes.
It is good to share, we say.

One by one
each of us adds our own

small and pointless contribution
until the music stops.

Now the parcel is so heavy
nobody can lift it anymore.

No matter.

It has learned how to grow
without our help.

We leave despair
in the centre
of the circle and stare at it.

It does nothing.
It is not ashamed.

It stares right back at us
from one huge screaming eye.

Remains – Berlin 1945

'I think of the effort of history to make connections and to remember'
  – Yehuda Amichai

I

There is only so much you can burn
without sufficient fuel
and even then

        Teeth

                Porcelain

         Gold fillings

                  the harder bones

tend to resist

        and need to be bludgeoned to powder

Tricky

II

What nation doesn't have its rites and rituals,
building plans, bridges, temples?

Who wouldn't make a burial ground
a pyramid, a pit, an oven?

The dead must be managed
to protect the living

This is rudimentary hygiene

III

At first a mad wind
birthed from the hell fires of Berlin

and they could not ignite
the shuddering match to set alight
    the corpses
drenched in whatever petrol they could muster

A torch from a twist of paper
    somebody said

        then finally ignition
            and a hasty *heil* from acolytes

who dared not linger
fearful of Russian shells

IV

What am I doing?

Do I really want to tell you
    do you really want to know
    the Red Army retrieved
    enough teeth
from a crater near the bunker
    to identify the führer's bite

upper-jaw bridgework

            genuine porcelain inlays

    a lower jawbone

V

Sometimes burning is hiding

The soul is a flame they say

Enough flames
and you imagine
you can burn
a world of history down

20264

After 'Mother with Baby' – Israel 1951, Ruth Orkin

And all you can do is rejoice at
the sight of them, captured here
chest to chest in the classic hold,
mother's right hand supporting
her baby's neck; all you can do
is delight in the mother's half-smile,
her big hair and her triumph, all
you can do is soften at the bald patch
at the back of the baby's skull,
the delicious curve of shoulder,
the gathered promise of the new.

The mother, you might note,
is not with you as you are with her;
she is glancing at something or
someone off camera, but if you let
your gaze drift towards the lower part
of the frame, where the baby's
tiny immensity rests on the mother's
left wrist, you will notice a row
of numbers on the mother's forearm
tattooed large, the right way up
for quick inspection: so easy to read.

is the madness caused by the poetry or is the poetry caused by the madness

in freefall
amid treatise and denial
where is the ground

which way up am I
lost in my own barrage
of em-dash and return and

other comparable
inky braking mechanisms
home comforts of my art

wait what is this
strange tense
I'm living in

who can even remember
the heady days
of wisdom and resolution

where once it was
the way of the poet
to reach for a point

of pause
to gather
if not stillness

silence perhaps
when this thing ends
god when will it ever

The News and the Blackbird

For days I've been nothing
but important to myself
writing this warring world
denying the distraction
of blackbird outside
my window, blackbird
who will not stop her song
who has no business here
and cannot know my pain –
and I don't know where
my eyes have been except
elsewhere and weeping,
my mind twisting open
like a fruit that won't
release its stone, my heart
grieving and beating
in the orchards of war.
But today the blackbird
sang suddenly in the key
of joy: *Look out! Look up!*
and what else could I do
but obey as she folded
into the green desire
of plum tree, home
to her nest that lay
hidden, chick-heavy
and ravenous behind
a celebration of leaves.

FOUR
ARBAH

עִבְרָא

'Your question, your answer.
Your song, what does it know?'
   – Paul Celan

Lox

Sunday mornings we'd stop for salmon ends at Cohen's
kosher temple of the flesh we could not afford
while wives bound in fur, wig and stocking, a kind of kin
ordered fish sliced thin on marble countertops
by sharp men who sold us the waste for next to nothing.
The taste is sweetest close to the skin, my mother whispered.
      A lifetime gone and secret salt still singing on my tongue.

Shmattes

These are the rags our foremothers and forefathers
pieced together like prayers in the murk of sweatshops

scraps they schlepped from door to door to earn
something out of nothing   manna for the survivor

food for the kinder who lived to beget my ancestors
of long buried names who begat nevertheless

my great grandmother Sheyna who conjured
by her own hand a yellow dress that caught

the eye of Jack the nice Jewish doctor who married
my grandmother Bessie the Communist who begat

Adrian   Robert   Felicity   and my own mother
Marna the teacher who did not care a button

for the tailor's art but begat me   Yael   I who can
write this poem but barely fix a shmatte to a shmatte

I who begat Jacob   Tamar   Ethan   Melissa
and therefore by the covenant of these pages

bless and remember   the yellow dress   the thread
the needle   the thimble   luck   feet   donkeys

carts   tracks   trains   courage of crossings
through loss   through fear and storm   the fruit

of the labour   fruit of the dreamer   fruit of the chutzpah
that has kept us alive and brought us to this season.

Madagascar

'The desirable solution is: all Jews out of Europe'
  – Franz Rademacher, July 1940

because there is a question and somebody must answer it
because it is our dream to banish parasites and criminals
because we have the means to commandeer transport
because there will be no question of long term liability
because accommodation where provided will be temporary
because the absence of infrastructure will not be scrutinised
because we consider the conditions suitably inhospitable
because the terrain will be hostile and the governance brutal
because the foreigners will be rendered stateless and stranded
because neither allies nor enemies will desire us to desist
because colonised Africa will relieve Europe of its burden
        because nobody else wants them

Mezze with Ethics

During the terrible mezze with its various
pretentions, Meg and I debate whether
humans can be divided into two categories:
suppose some are born incapable of love;
maybe they are another species, maybe
there's nothing we can do about that, let alone
this appalling aubergine of despair.
Empathy is a burden we carry, I tell my friend,
washing it down with water, smug that
this constant pain, this inability to swallow
somehow absolves me. I don't know Meg,
I opine as I chew the slimy mozzarella,
even Hitler was devoted to his dog
before he poisoned him, even Frau Goebbels
loved her children when she killed them,
even I might put a bullet in Putin or Bolsonaro
if you gave me some lessons and a gun.
Meanwhile the taramasalata has congealed
and the despicable beans have given up hope
but when the sad waiter tenders the bill
(*the war, the drought, the price of fuel and fertiliser*)
I remember I am not hungry and I say nothing.

Mazel

for Robin

We seize it like ice-cream in summer, like
love when you're lonely, like kiss-me-again,
like sex, like time, like home, like taking
the corners of this wide life over and over
while we still can. The blinds rise to *mazel*
as they let in the light, the summer shines it
in sky-shades of forget-me-not, a son brews it
in the blessing of morning coffee; a daughter
carries *mazel* home, baked into hot bread
from the floury queue at The Dusty Knuckle;
a woman at the beach car park offers *mazel*
winding down the window of her Ford Fiesta
with the gift of a free dashboard ticket
to a beautiful day going nowhere; and on
towel-striped sands, a stranger tosses cones
of *mazel* from a box of melting Cornettos
because *no way can I eat them all myself*;
and talking of self and melt, a person can be
mazel too, like you are now, chancing in
with your smile on show as I write this poem;
the way your cheeks round like small pink plums,
your head tilts a little to the left like always,
your eyes say *mensch, mensch*, sand and years,
kiss-me-again, forget-me-never and *mazel, mazel,*
mazel tov, another day rounding another corner.

Peace be Upon You

'Every one of us is a fiddler on the roof trying to scratch
out a pleasant, simple tune without breaking his neck'
– Tevye, Fiddler on the Roof

Mandatory like mothers or doctors
or herring, there were violin lessons,
classical and klezmer dredged from
the mass graves of Europe in rituals
of horsehair and resin, the old stories
disinterred from forests, rising
from velvet, catgut and rosewood.
What Jewish parent would not stick
Chagall's *Violiniste Vert* to the door
of a refrigerator, or would not kvell
to say *My kid the fiddle player*, or
would not speak in tones of awe
of Haifetz, Oistrakh, Menuhin?

It is no easy task to coax a song
from the instrument; I won't say
I was good, but once or twice
I felt history's river bless my hands
as I drew the bow across the strings
and entered the dreamscape of
Sholem Aleichem, he who kept alive
the shtetl of the mind. Play on,
he told me, don't forget: sometimes
there was a hat, often a homecoming,
a wedding, a pogrom, a farewell –
and now and then a crazy musician
balanced on a rooftop above a village
nobody remembers, playing the violin.

Jankel

I never knew you Jack, or was it Jankel
but they named me after you. I heard you stank
of shtetl Jack, your accent made them call you
Jew. You never ditched your Litvak twang
my mother said. Your brothers with the knack
for shekls took you to the bank, bought you a desk
a white coat and a stethoscope, made you Dr. Jack.
Oh Grandpa Jack, you crazy Stalinist, caught
on camera with the red flag, Edinburgh, May Day
nineteen-thirty-two, you leftist hack, the man
whose eyes were sad and black, who knows
what you'd been through? You left me clues:
this, your scratched consulting desk, a streak
of melancholy, tracks of dust and sepia, your name.
These words are all that I can give you back.

1939

And it is said that in the year 5699 my grandmother Bessie Greenstein (née Yawitch) travelled to Lithuania with her brother-in-law Max Greenstein and his wife Lilly Greenstein, known to the family as Diamond Lil.

We do not know where exactly they went or why, whether they knew this was the last chance. We do not know the names of the Greenstein relatives they were visiting who had once lived, it is said, in the shtetl known as Aniksht.

On this, the records are silent.

Druch was the name from which my great grandmother Levi was descended according to my grandmother's birth certificate. But names slip. And graves slip and stones fall and history vanishes. My Uncle believes my great Grandmother was Sheyna Lipshe. My grandmother's birth certificate names her as Levi Druch.

It is said that while in Lithuania, Bessie received a phone call from my grandfather, Dr Jack who was studying at the Hammersmith Hospital in London. He told her to return to England with all haste. We speculate, or so it has been handed down, that German physicians, colleagues of my grandfather, warned Dr Jack that a German invasion was imminent.

We do not know how the German physicians knew this.

Or why they would have risked the telling.

We would like to believe that they were good people.

But on this, the records are silent.

We know – or so the story goes, that when the phone call was finished, the operator, who had listened to all of it, asked if everything would be alright. *And what could I say?* my grandmother commented later.

We know – although again this is hearsay – that three lucky Jews, Granny Bessie, Max and Diamond Lil immediately boarded a train and crossed the borders of Germany, Belgium and France.

And the story goes that as the train rolled across Northern Germany, the guard, checking their travel documents, commented *What wouldn't I give to have one of these.*

And it is told by my uncle that only two days after their return to England, on the 17th of Elul, 5699, Germany invaded Poland.

We know that shortly thereafter my grandmother, Max and Lily and Jack boarded a ship and voyaged back to Cape Town.

And it is said that only one Lithuanian relative, Jascha Gurewits, survived. We assume also that the rest, whoever they were – who were they? – perished in the Shoah.

We do not know their names.

May there be abundant peace from heaven.

We do not, we will not, imagine the extent of the pain my grandmother lived with for the rest of her days. Who did she leave behind? She rarely spoke of them. She never named them. We never asked.

We know that my grandmother refused to set foot on German soil all the days of her life. That my mother in her turn, and I in my turn, refused to go there, that when I found myself on a plane diverted to Frankfurt due to bad weather, terror struck my heart.

Legend tells that my grandmother, blessed with two children before the Shoah, chose to wait until after the war before completing her family.

But my aunt, Felicity was born in Tamus 5705 (July 1945) – conceived before Germany's defeat. Did my grandmother have intelligence that the tide was turning? Or was this new life created out of an ancient imperative to be fruitful and multiply in the face of genocide?

On this, and this, and all that, so much, the records are silent.

The Trains, Again

for Imogen and Wanda

Passover: the apple tree in her mother's garden
is big with blossom, and my friend whose mother
reprised for us *Chad Gadya* in Ladino, my friend
of fifty years, my friend whose mother handed down
to us her recipe for quajado, my friend whose mother
was once kissed by Mussolini – *Bella Bambina!* –
my friend whose mother wore the yellow star
my friend whose mother fled and lived, my friend
whose relatives were taken far away from home
and never came back, my friend who weeps with me
over railways and refugees, the newly displaced
disgorged at Berlin Hauptbahnhof, the war, the trains
again the trains, it is this friend whose mother told her
        That is the tree, that is the tree
– as she chopped the onions, stirred the soup
bleached the bleachable, celebrated the spring:
When they come for us, I will hang myself from that tree.

      When will they come for us, my friend?
      Can you hear the trains? I hear them
      in my sleep, rattling continents, heaving
      and breathing along the tracks of my veins
      riding my blood. There is no silencing them.

Love

So much hangs
on the word
yet it keeps on walking.

Loaded
with our longings
upwards it trudges.

The word is not blinkered;
its wide eyes
know no night.

We feed it with faith
and it eats
as it climbs

eternal spine braced
under the weight
of promises.

I love you:
easy to say.
Love shrugs

as in *forever*
or *whatever*
or *sure, Honey*

and sniffs the air.
Another fire
is on the way.

Love takes the heat.
Puts one foot
in front of the other.

Notes

'Do not be daunted by the enormity of the world's grief. Do justly, now. Walk humbly, now. You are not obligated to complete the work, but neither are you free to abandon it.' Rabbi Tarfon in the *Pirkei Avot* which translates as *Laws of the Fathers* – although I prefer *Laws of the Ancestors*. The Pirkei Avot forms part of the Mishnah, the first text of Jewish oral law.

Tomaszów Lubelski
Tomaszów Lubelski, the home of my paternal grandparents is a town in North-eastern Poland. Many of the Jews, including members of my family, chose to go east with the Russians to Siberia rather than wait for the Germans, who occupied the town in the early stages of the war. The Germans established a Jewish ghetto and from there they transported the Jews to the nearby town of Belzec where they had built an extermination camp.

i can't go back / wherever i came from / was burned off the map
From *Notes of an Immigrant Daughter* by Melanie Kaye who was born in Brooklyn, New York in 1945. Later known as Melanie Kaye/ Kantrowitz, she was an activist, campaigner and writer.

Other Jews in the area
Shofar – a ram's horn blown a hundred times at Rosh Hashanah (New Year) services and blown just once to mark the end of the fast day on Yom Kippur (the Day of Atonement).

Shmattes are literally rags or ragged clothes but can also refer to the clothing business or 'rag trade'.

Oświęcim
Oświęcim is the Polish name for Auschwitz.

And my scream is made of strange edges / like a complicated key
From *Try Again* by Yehuda Amichai who was born in Germany in 1924. Amichai was one of Israel's finest poets. He said "… real poems deal with a human response to reality, and politics is part of reality, history in making."

Overheard on a Train 1, 2 and 3
Found poems based on notes taken of an overheard conversation on a return train journey from Euston to Northampton in November 2022 during my failed attempt to travel to the climate conference, COP 26 in Glasgow.

The Plagues are Everywhere
This was written during the first Covid lockdown where family and friends attempted a Passover meal and service on Zoom. Passover is my favourite festival: a raucous, argumentative and musical celebration of springtime, renewal and freedom where we read the story of the Exodus of Jews from Egypt. Part of the service recounts the ten plagues visited by God onto the Egyptians to force them to free the Jews from slavery.

The plate referred to is the Seder (Passover service) plate where ritual foods are placed. Ours, a gift from my Uncle Robert and decorated with blue birds, is a replica of a plate confiscated by the Nazis for their planned 'Museum to an Extinct Race'.

Going to Bed with Hitler
This poem was written in response to my experience of reading *Hitler: Volume I: Ascent 1889-1939* (Vintage, 2017) *and and Hitler: Volume II: Downfall (1939-45)* by Volker Ullrich (Bodley Head, 2020) both translated from the German by Jefferson Chase.

I don't need any; I live like a bird in the wild
From Hitler's speech in 1932 after an expenses scandal.

The sky was hung with violins …I had not a care in the world
From a recollection by Hitler in 1942.

Burn down their synagogues. Toss them in fire and pitch. Throw in some hellfire!
Adapted from Martin Luther's work *The Jews and their Lies*, 1543.

Aniksht was a town in North-eastern Lithuania that my mother's father and family came from (as far as we know).

The greatest moment of my life! Hitler on Napoleon whom he regarded as a role model and kindred spirit.

The entire people love him, because it feels safe in his hands like a child in the arms of its mother and *Magnificent how the people are awakening.* From the diary of Josef Goebbels.

His face was grey as ashes; his hands were in a constant state of agitation. He was bent over like an old man. From the post-war testimony of Ilse Braun, sister of Eva Braun.

The scream of the twelve-inch shrapnel is more penetrating than the hiss from a thousand Jewish newspaper vipers! From *Mein Kampf.*

The Trial
In a German court, 93 year old Bruno Dey, a former SS Concentration camp guard, was found guilty of complicity in the murder of 5000 prisoners in Stutthof Concentration Camp. He was given a two-year suspended sentence.

Death could drop from the dark / As easily as song
From *Returning, We Hear the Larks* by Isaac Rosenberg who wrote some of the finest poems of World War One and was killed on active service in March 1918.

Velvel's Violin
This poem is loosely based on the testimony of Rachel Shtibel, a Holocaust survivor who wrote *The Violin*, a memoir of her experiences. "I know they're proud of me that I remember and that I tell the world what happened" she said.

Madagascar
Originally, before their decision to murder the Jews, the Germans planned to transport them to Madagascar on boats they would requisition following an expected naval victory over Great Britain. That victory never happened. Africa seems to be a popular choice of destination for getting rid of unwanted populations: "I would love to have a front page of *The Telegraph* with a plane taking off to Rwanda, that's my dream, it's my obsession" – Suella Braverman, UK Home Secretary, October 2022.

Your question, your answer. / Your song, what does it know?
From *Keine Sandkunst mehr / No More SandArt* by Paul Celan, the acclaimed German Jewish poet whose family were murdered during the war. He survived but suffered from debilitating depression. He killed himself in 1970.

Mazel
Mazel – luck of the happy kind.

Peace be Upon You
The violin was a popular instrument in Eastern European Jewish culture. Jews were forbidden to take up most professions but musician was not one of them. For the few prodigies, becoming a violinist was a route out of the grinding poverty of the shtetl and a chance to travel. Sholem Aleichem (variant of a phrase that translates as *peace be upon you*) was the pen name of Solomon Naumovich Rabinowich Aleichem (1959-1916), a Yiddish author and playwright. The musical *Fiddler on the Roof* was based on his (much darker) stories of Tevye the Dairyman.

1939
The dates in this poem are based on the Jewish calendar which uses a lunisolar system. There are different opinions as to the starting date of the calendar, but it is broadly considered to denote the years since creation.

The Trains, Again
Chad Gadya – *One Little Goat* is a cumulative song traditionally sung towards the end of the Passover ritual when a great deal of wine has been consumed.

Quajado is a Sephardi omelette made with leeks. It's delicious!

Berlin Hauptbahnhof is the central station in Berlin. During the early part of Russia's war on Ukraine in 2022, thousands of refugees arrived by train every day.

Acknowledgements and Thanks

Family, both present and past is a big part of this book. Thanks to Robin for love, literary support and breakfasts; to Tamar, my personal dramaturg for helping me to organise the first draft of the manuscript; to Melissa for telling me I ate and left no crumbs; to Ethan and Jacob for inspiration, hugs and encouragement. Thanks to Uncle Robbie for the memories and the stories.

Immense gratitude to my poet tribe and friends for critiques, conversations, challenges, debates: especially Anja Konig, Norbert Hirschhorn, Sophie Herxheimer, Miriam Nash, Tamar Yoseloff, Tom Sastry, Aviva Dautch, Sasha Dugdale, Alex Abraham, Imogen Barford, Anna Veprinska.

Thank you to Imogen Barford and Peter Wakefield for providing retreat and sanctuary in Suffolk. And thank you to Joe Warner for being my on-demand film maker and cheering me on.

Thanks forever to Jane Commane at Nine Arches Press for her poet's heart and her persistent, challenging and inspiring editing.

Gratitude to the following publications in which versions of some of the poems in this book first appeared: *Poetry Wales, Plough Magazine, Poetry Birmingham Literary Journal, Fourteen Magazine, Bad Lilies, Ink Sweat & Tears.*

'Yom Kippur' was commended in the Troubadour Poetry Competition. 'Before the War' was commissioned by The Poetry Society and the EU National Institutes for Culture and was the result of a collaboration with poet Nora Nadjarian. 'The Trial' and 'The Plagues are Everywhere' previously appeared in *One Hundred Lockdown Sonnets* (Nine Arches Press, 2021) and 'Jankel' previously appeared in *The Kitchen of Lovely Contraptions* (flipped eye, 2011).